What is
the Bible?

Basics of the Faith

Sean Michael Lucas, Series Editor

What Is the Bible?

Guy Prentiss Waters

P&R PUBLISHING

P.O. BOX 817 • PHILLIPSBURG • NEW JERSEY 08865-0817

ISBN: 978-1-59638-711-9 (pbk)
ISBN: 978-1-59638-712-6 (ePub)
ISBN: 978-1-59638-713-3 (Mobi)

Page design by Tobias Design

Printed in the United States of America

Library of Congress Cataloging-in-Publication Data

Waters, Guy Prentiss, 1975-
  What is the Bible? / Guy Prentiss Waters.
    pages cm. -- (Basics of the faith)
  Includes bibliographical references.
  ISBN 978-1-59638-711-9 (pbk.)
  1. Bible--Introductions. I. Title.
  BS475.3.W38 2013
  220.6'1--dc23
                    2013023464

□ "Yea, hath God said . . .?" (Gen. 3:1 AV).

And so the whole sad affair began. When the Devil wanted to draw Adam and Eve into sin, he began with a question. Not just any question. It was a question designed to throw Eve on her heels. It was a question that would go on purposefully to distort God's earlier words to Adam (Gen. 3:2 with Gen. 2:16–17), and would eventually lead to Satan's bald contradiction of God, "You will not surely die" (Gen. 3:4). Satan was working hard to sow doubt in, to distort, and to deny the Word of God. He knew that if he could persuade Adam and Eve to cast off the mantle of divine authority, he could win them. He was right.

Thankfully that was not the end of the story. In pronouncing his curse upon the serpent, God announced his intention to send a Redeemer—born of Eve no less—who would crush Satan's head and whose heel would be bruised in the process (Gen. 3:15). Adam and Eve, and many others since, believed in that divine promise. We have seen that promise come to fruition at the cross (Col. 2:13–15), and will witness its full realization on the day that Jesus returns in glory (Rev. 20:7–10).

Until then the Devil is staying busy. Very busy. His hatred of Christians is unalloyed and unrelenting. He would love nothing more than for professing Christians to share in his everlasting and certain misery. For this reason Peter warns us to "be watchful" (1 Peter 5:8). Christians need to be vigilant, but we also need to remember, as Martin Luther said, that the Devil is "God's devil." God is sovereign over the Devil who is but his creature. Christ has triumphed over the Devil at the cross. Scripture calls Christians to "resist the devil, and he will flee" from us (James 4:7).

So how do we resist the Devil? Paul commands us to "put on the whole armor of God, that you may be able to stand against the schemes of the devil" (Eph. 6:11). What goes into the Christian armament? The "belt of truth" and the "sword of the Spirit, which is the word of God" (Eph. 6:14, 17). Remember how Luther calls us to sing in his famous hymn "A Mighty Fortress Is Our God."

> The Prince of Darkness grim, we tremble not for him;
> His rage we can endure, for lo, his doom is sure,
> One little word shall fell him.

What does all this have to do with Scripture? Everything. You and I and every other Christian are in the fight of our lives, and this fight has eternal consequences. We fight confidently because we know that no true Christian will lose this fight. Even so, we do not fight presumptuously. We use all the means that God has appointed for our warfare. One of those means is the Scripture, the Word of God. The better we get to know the Word of God, the more effectively we can wield it in battle. The more confidence we have in the Bible as the Word of God, the more confidently we will wage the fight in which we now find ourselves.

The precious truth that the Bible is the Word of God has long been the church's settled conviction. In the last couple of centuries, however, a cacophony of voices from within the visible church has questioned—even denied—this proposition. The practical consequences have been devastating. As J. I. Packer has observed, loss of confidence in the full divine authority of the Bible in the Protestant church has "undermined preaching," "undercut teaching," "weakened faith," "discouraged lay Bible reading," and "hidden Christ from view."[1] These grim outcomes undoubtedly delight the Devil. They serve to remind us of the importance of all Christians—church officers and non–church officers alike—having clear, distinct, and accurate views concerning the Bible's teaching about itself.

GETTING A HANDLE ON THE WORD OF GOD

So just what is the Bible? Is the Bible simply a collection of the elevated religious reflections of holy men and women that God subsequently approved and called his own, or did God have something to do with the Bible's production? If that's the case, then how can we speak of the Bible as written both by God and by man? Did God write part of it or all of it? Haven't people claimed that there are errors and contradictions in the Bible? Can a twenty-first-century individual *really* be expected to submit his or her life to a book that was written millennia ago and half a world away?

In what follows, we are going to try to address these questions and more. To come to terms with what the Bible is, we are going to think about three terms—*revelation*, *inspiration*, and *inerrancy*. These terms either come from the Bible itself or summarize the Bible's teaching about itself. Once we understand these terms, we will be able to think about how to prepare ourselves to answer some of the objections raised against the Bible in our own day.

DEFINITIONS

Revelation

Sometimes an idea dawns on us and we tell a friend, "I had a revelation!" We often use the word in connection with experiences that are sudden, unexpected, or particularly insightful. This is not an unacceptable way of speaking, of course, but it does not capture what the church has meant when it claims that the Bible is *revelation*.

At the heart of the idea of revelation, biblically speaking, is disclosure. In fact the English word *reveal* comes from a Latin verb meaning "to pull back the veil." Revelation suggests a revealer, something revealed, and recipients of revelation. God is the revealer, sovereignly choosing to make something known. He is lifting the veil, as it were, to show us humans something we could not have found out on our own. The matters that God thus discloses we may term *revelation*. To speak of revelation, then, is to speak of a living, personal God who communicates truth to his rational creatures.[2] This truth supremely concerns God himself— "his nature, works, will, or purposes."[3]

Theologians distinguish two kinds of revelation. One is called *natural* or *general* revelation. The other is called *special revelation*. Both are revelation in the sense that we have described above. Each, however, is distinct in its content and in its purposes.

General Revelation. The first kind of revelation is called *natural* or *general*. The term *natural* refers to the fact that this revelation comes through nature, the works of God's hands. The term *general* refers to the fact that this revelation is general in scope—all human beings are its recipients.

General revelation is God's disclosure of himself through the created order.

Paul speaks of this revelation in his epistle to the Romans:

> For what can be known about God is plain to [men], because God has shown it to them. For his invisible attributes, namely, his eternal power and divine nature, have been clearly perceived, ever since the creation of the world, in the things that have been made. So they are without excuse. (1:19–20)

Notice what Paul says here. God is revealing himself through the works of his hands. His wisdom, goodness, and power are evident throughout the created order. No wonder the psalmist cries out, "The heavens declare the glory of God" (Ps. 19:1). God also reveals himself in such a way that the message gets through to people. The revelation is "plain" just because God "has shown it" to men. All people, therefore, are "without excuse." No one will stand before God on the day of judgment and tell him, "I did not know of your existence." The whole universe—from subatomic particles to entire galaxies—will be prepared to testify against that person. What Paul is saying, furthermore, is true not simply in his generation but for all time. God's self-revelation through the creation has been going on "ever since the creation of the world."

As glorious as this revelation is, we may speak biblically of two limitations to general revelation. One concerns its content. The other concerns its purpose. General revelation ineluctably tells us many wonderful, true things about the God who made and sustains the universe. One thing it does not tell us is how a sinner may be saved. When it comes to the saving mercies of God, the creation is mute. This silence is no flaw of general revelation. In fact, this is precisely what God has intended general revelation to be. Why is this so? It is because one leading purpose of general revelation is to leave the sinner inexcusable. Mind and conscience constantly testify to the existence of God and of his righteous law (see Rom. 2:14–15). General revelation reminds us that there is coming a final and full outpouring of the wrath of a holy and just God (Rom. 1:18). On that day, there will be nothing for the unpardoned sinner to do except to close his mouth and to bow his knee before the Divine Majesty.

Special Revelation. Thankfully, general revelation is not the only revelation God gives to humanity. We may also speak of *special revelation.* What makes special revelation, well, special? We may point to two matters. First, special revelation addresses people as sinners, and tells them what they need to know of God and of his will in order to be saved.[4] Special revelation builds upon general revelation by disclosing matters otherwise unrevealed and unavailable to our minds. General revelation is simply insufficient to tell the sinner what he needs to know in order to be saved. Special revelation, however, neither replaces nor corrects general revelation. On the contrary, without general revelation as its context, special revelation would make little sense. The nineteenth-century Presbyterian biblical scholar and theologian B. B. Warfield captures the relationship between general revelation and special revelation when he says, "They do not stand as two systems, each complete in itself, over against one another; but together they form one organic whole."[5] Special revelation is different from general revelation in a second sense. As we saw Paul teach in Romans 1, general revelation is available to every human being since the creation of the world. Special revelation is available only to certain persons. One of Israel's privileges during the Old Testament era was that God had uniquely revealed himself to her.

> He declares his word to Jacob,
>> his statutes and rules to Israel.
> He has not dealt thus with any other nation;
>> they do not know his rules.
> Praise the LORD! (Ps. 147:19–20; see also Rom. 3:2)

This revelation, as the psalmist recognizes, was a gracious act of God who is worthy to be praised. Furthermore, Israel was not supposed to hoard up what she knew, but to diffuse the light of God's revelation to the nations around her (Deut. 4:1–8). Today, under the new covenant, the special saving knowledge of God has gone to the nations by the command of God (see Isa. 49:6; Matt. 28:18–20). This is why Christians have worked long and hard to translate the Scriptures and to distribute Bibles across the globe. Sadly, not every person in the world today has access to a Bible. Even today not every human being has access to special revelation.

What may we say of special revelation itself? First, the focus and concern of special revelation is the salvation of the sinner. Put another way, special revelation is designed to inform sinners how the communion and fellowship between God and man, severed at the fall, may be restored in Jesus Christ. Put yet another way, special revelation shows us how God has purposed to glorify his mercy and his justice through the salvation of fallen men and women. To be sure, special revelation does more than simply convey information. It also summons men and women to repentance and faith in Jesus Christ. Special revelation, however, is not less than the conveyance of information. Without it, people ordinarily cannot be saved.[6]

Special revelation has come through various modes. When we read the Old Testament, we sometimes see God communicating with people through miracles, dreams, visions, and angelic visitations. We should not think, however, that God spoke to his people only in such extraordinary fashion. God also revealed himself in letters, songs of praise, and historical narratives. Much of the Bible, in fact, falls into this latter category.[7]

Special revelation did not come all at once. God progressively revealed himself to his people. This revelation found its goal, its fulfillment, in Jesus Christ, who is the Word of God (John 1:1, 18). The writer of the epistle to the Hebrews succinctly states the point: "Long ago, at many times and in many ways, God spoke to our fathers by the prophets, but in these last days he has spoken to us by his Son" (Heb. 1:1–2).

This point helps us to understand our Bible. The Bible has a single message. That single message runs straight from Genesis to Revelation. For all its wondrous diversity, the Bible never goes "off message." This message centers upon God's plan to redeem sinners through his Son. We first encounter it in Genesis 3:15, what some have called the *protoevangelium*, which is a Latin word meaning "the first announcement of the gospel." And that message stays with us until the closing words of the Bible: "The grace of the Lord Jesus be with all. Amen" (Rev. 22:21). This unity of message is why Jesus himself can tell the Jews that the Scriptures "bear witness about me" (John 5:39), and his disciples that the message of the Old Testament was nothing other than the message of his person and work (see Luke 24:26–27, 44–49). The Bible is not cacophonic but symphonic.

Special revelation is progressive and fundamentally redemptive in character. When we attend carefully to its contours, something interesting emerges. There is a certain pattern to this revelation. It is a pattern of "redemptive deed" and "redemptive word." So often in the Bible, we read of God doing a great redemptive act. Think of the exodus or Israel's restoration from her exile in Babylon. This great redemptive act is often attended by a word that interprets how the act is redemptive. That is to say, God goes to great lengths to help his people understand what his works in redemptive history mean for them and for others.[8] There is a kind of clustering to special revelation. Special revelation clusters around great works of God in redemptive history. The Pentateuch, or the first five books of the Old Testament, centers around the exodus, or God's great redemption of Israel from her Egyptian bondage. We later see many prophets writing around the time of Israel's exile into Babylon and of Israel's restoration seventy years later. The greatest example of this clustering principle, however, is the New Testament itself. All twenty-seven books of the New Testament explain and interpret the greatest of God's redemptive deeds in history—the humiliation and exaltation of the Lord Jesus Christ.

Inspiration

Christians have long affirmed the Bible to be an inspired book. The Westminster Confession of Faith, for instance, claims that the sixty-six books of the Bible are "all . . . given by inspiration of God to be the rule of faith and life."[9] The founding documents of the Church of England make similar claims.[10] These are but two examples of a universal commitment to the inspiration of the Bible.

But what are we saying when we claim that the Bible is *inspired*? The term is admittedly subject to misunderstanding. Our minds might turn to something that inspires or motivates us. I find, for instance, the experience of listening to J. S. Bach's Fifth Brandenburg Concerto or John Coltrane's "Giant Steps" to be moving and motivating—inspirational, some might say.

When we say that the Bible is *inspired*, however, we are not talking about the effect or impact that the Bible has on us. We are making a claim about what the Bible is. To be sure, the Bible should be and often has been transformational and life changing. That is not what we mean by *inspiration*.

Another way that the word *inspiration* can be misunderstood has to do with the root meaning of the word. Broken down into its parts, *inspired* means "breathed into." Inspiration might suggest that God took an existing set of books and claimed them for himself, saying, "Now these are *mine*." But that is not what the doctrine of inspiration says. The doctrine says that, as their author, God produced the books that we call *inspired*.

Where did the term *inspired* originate, anyway? It comes from the venerable Authorized Version's translation of Paul's words to Timothy in 2 Timothy 3:16, "All scripture is given by inspiration of God . . ." The Greek word underlying the English translation "by inspiration of God" has been more precisely translated "breathed out by God."[11] The idea is not that God breathed into something that already existed, as the Authorized Version might suggest. The idea, J. I. Packer observes, is that "just as God made the host of heaven 'by the breath of his mouth' (Ps. 33:6), through His own creative fiat, so we should regard the Scriptures as the product of a similar creative fiat."[12] This biblical phrase "breathed out by God" commits us, then, to a very high view of the Scripture indeed. Provided we understand the term *inspired* in this fashion, it should remain part of our Christian vocabulary.

On the face of it, *revelation* and *inspiration* seem to be similar if not identical terms. They are, however, distinct terms. *Revelation* denotes God self-disclosing truths to humanity. In special revelation, we have seen, God discloses himself through human instruments. *Inspiration*, however, denotes a work of God—"his providential, gracious, and supernatural contributions being presupposed"—within the human writers of Scripture "in their entire work of writing, with the design and effect of rendering the written product the divinely trustworthy Word of God."[13] Put another way, revelation tells us that God is disclosing himself in words to people; inspiration tells us that this written product is nothing less or other than *God's* Word.

Paul claims that "all Scripture" is *inspired*. To what does Paul refer when he speaks of "all Scripture"? In the previous verse he speaks of "the sacred writings, which are able to make you wise for salvation through faith in Christ Jesus" (2 Tim. 3:15). These writings are the books of the Old Testament. Paul is saying that the entirety of the Old Testament ("all Scripture") is "breathed out by God."

The apostle Peter says something similar at 2 Peter 1:21, "For no prophecy was ever produced by the will of man, but men spoke from God as they were carried along by the Holy Spirit." In view is biblical prophecy, particularly Old Testament prophecy (see 2 Peter 1:19–20). Peter, furthermore, is speaking categorically. What he affirms he affirms of *all* Old Testament prophecy.[14] Prophecy does not have its origin, Peter says, in the will of man. Prophecy, though, has come by men. Peter explains that "men spoke from God as they were carried along by the Holy Spirit." Warfield summarizes Peter's point: "Speaking thus under the determining influence of the Holy Spirit, the things [the prophets] spoke were not from themselves, but from God."[15]

What about the books of the New Testament? During his earthly ministry, Jesus appointed the apostles as those who would found the church in her new covenant form (see Matt. 16:13–20; Eph. 2:20). In the upper room, Christ told them that he would, by the Spirit, call to their minds the things that he had spoken to them (John 14:26). He also told them that there were new matters that he would reveal to them by the Holy Spirit—matters which they were not presently prepared to receive (John 16:12–15). These promises found their fulfillment in the books of the New Testament.[16] How do the apostles tell us to regard these new books? They instruct us to regard them as having the same authority as the books of the Old Testament. Thus Paul can quote a passage from Luke's gospel immediately after a passage from Deuteronomy, introducing them both with the statement, "For the Scripture says . . ." (1 Tim. 5:18). Peter can speak of individuals twisting the letters of Paul "as they do the other Scriptures" (2 Peter 3:16).[17] Under the new covenant, then, we have an expansion of the canon of Scripture. It is the apostles, authoritatively commissioned by Christ, who oversee this expansion. The apostles not only confirm that the Old Testament is the inspired Word of God, but instruct the church to regard the books of the New Testament as having precisely the same authority as the books of the Old Testament. The unbroken testimony of the apostles is that the books of both Testaments are in their entirety special revelation, the inspired Word of God.

We could multiply dozens of passages to demonstrate the same point—what God spoke through the instrumentality of human writers is nothing less than his Divine Word.[18] Following the Scripture, theologians therefore speak of the *plenary, verbal inspiration of Scripture.* By *plenary* we mean that "the whole of Scripture is given by divine inspiration."[19] That is to say, the whole of the Scripture, from beginning to end and inclusive of all its parts, is inspired. By *verbal* we mean that the inspiration of Scripture extends down to its very words. It is not enough to say that the thoughts or ideas of Scripture are inspired. To be true to the Scripture's testimony about itself, we must say that each word of the original was given by divine inspiration.[20]

So how are we to understand the interaction of the divine and the human in the production of Scripture? This question is admittedly a difficult one. Anytime we consider the interaction of the divine and the human, we must be prepared to acknowledge the limits of our understanding and to beware speculating beyond what God has revealed in Scripture.

We may say a couple of things. First, we are not saying that inspiration somehow obliterated the personality of the human author. Isaiah was still very much Isaiah when he wrote the prophecies under his name. Paul never ceased being Paul as he drafted each of his letters. Second, as J. I. Packer notes, we are not saying that inspiration "necessarily involve[d] an abnormal state of mind on the writer's part, such as a trance, or vision, or hearing a voice."[21] Sometimes the biblical writers *did* see a vision that they were commanded to write down. Often, however, the biblical writers did the difficult and demanding work of historical research (Luke 1:1–4).

The best way to understand this relationship is in terms of what theologians have called "God's *concursive* relationship in, with, and through the free working of man's own mind."[22]

What do theologians mean by *concursus* in this connection? They mean that God in his providence first created, shaped, and molded his intended writer. God so crafted the "mind, outlook, culture, language, and literary ability" of each writer that his "message . . . could always find adequate and exact expression."[23] This writer would freely and spontaneously produce the book of Scripture that God had purposed for him to write.[24] He may or may not have been aware that he was producing an inspired text.[25] One thing that was sure was that the Holy Spirit so completely governed, or superintended, the process as to ensure that the product was entirely God's Word (recall John 14:26; 16:12–15; see also 1 Cor 2:12–13). The result, therefore, is a Bible that is "divine-human . . . in which every word is at once divine and human."[26] Well then might we conclude with Warfield that "the Scriptures are throughout a Divine book, created by the Divine energy and speaking in their every part with Divine Authority directly to the heart of the readers . . . [and] the whole of it has been given by God through the instrumentality of men."[27]

Inerrancy

The words *inerrancy* and *infallibility* are often used to describe the Scripture. For most of church history, they were used more or less interchangeably. Within the last century, some theologians have claimed that the Bible is *infallible* but not *inerrant*.[28] Let us define each of these terms and see whether one or both appropriately describes the Bible.

The word *infallible* refers to "the quality of neither deceiving nor being deceived." The word *inerrant* means "freedom from error of any kind, factual, moral, or spiritual."[29] As John Frame observes, "*inerrant* means that there *are* no errors; *infallible* means that there *can be* no errors."[30] The two terms are very close in meaning, and it is difficult to see how one could cogently affirm the Bible to be *infallible* without also affirming it to be *inerrant*. If the Bible is incapable of deceiving us, it must be free from deceptions of any kind.

On what basis would we make such an affirmation about the Bible? After all, critics note, the word *inerrant* is never used by the biblical writers in describing the Scripture. This observation is true; however, inerrancy is a "necessary inference" from the character of God who produced the Bible, the Word of God.[31] This statement is an important one. Let us give a little attention to it.

The Bible, as we have seen, is a revelation from God, and was given by inspiration of God. It is in this sense that we confess the Bible to be the Word of God. What we know of the character of God will necessarily determine our understanding of the character of his Word. John Gerstner summarizes the point well.

> There are only two ways by which any person can come to say something that is untrue: either by ignorance or lying. . . . God suffers from neither limitation, and therefore cannot speak untruth. His message must be true indubitably. . . . God who is truth, who cannot err, has inspired the Bible, and the Bible is truth and cannot err.[32]

In other words, if the God who cannot lie has spoken, and if he has given us that Word by inspiration, then that Word cannot deceive and cannot be in error. It is both infallible and inerrant. Conversely, "to maintain that there are flaws or errors in [the Bible] is the same as declaring that there are flaws or errors in God Himself."[33] Some have objected to this argument.[34] It is illegitimate, they say, to deduce inerrancy in the manner that we have done. In the absence of an explicit biblical statement of its own inerrancy, we should not speak of the Scripture as *inerrant*.

This objection can stand for only one of two reasons. Either the particular deduction outlined above is invalid or deductions are altogether invalid.[35] To deny the validity of deductions is to destroy the foundations for much of what we know. But what of the former option? Is it illegitimate to deduce the inerrancy of Scripture from its divine inspiration? Based upon what we know of the character of God and of the character of his Word, inerrancy is an inescapable deduction. It is one on which we may stand with the strongest confidence.

"But," someone says, "what about all those errors and contradictions that people say are in the Bible? How can you claim that the Bible is inerrant in the face of those claims?" It is true that people have been claiming for a long time that the Bible contains errors and contradictions. On one level, this should not surprise us. The Devil, God's implacable enemy, is a "liar and the father of lies." His spiritual children choose "to do [their] father's desires" (John 8:44). The Devil and those allied with him love neither the God of truth nor the truth that God has spoken. It is no wonder that they should slander God and his Word.

That said, we need to take charges of error and contradiction with the utmost seriousness. We should not be dismissive of them or cavalier in our handling of them. We need, then, a strategy or approach in handling such charges.

To begin, we should bear in mind a couple of basic considerations when we enter into discussions like these. The first concerns the way in which we formulate our doctrine of Scripture. Some people try to build a doctrine of Scripture in the wrong way. They do not begin with the Bible's own statements about itself; namely, that it is the inspired Word of God, and therefore inerrant. They begin, rather, with passages that present difficulties to them. They proceed on that basis to form an understanding of the nature of the Scripture.

What is wrong with this approach? As Warfield has noted, it is "a settled logical principle that so long as the proper evidence by which a proposition is established remains unrefuted, all so-called objections brought against it pass out of the category of objections to its truth into the category of difficulties to be adjusted to it."[36] What is Warfield saying? He is saying that the case for an inspired and therefore inerrant Bible is settled and irrefutable.[37] If this case is sound, then we may have a well-grounded commitment to an inspired and inerrant Bible. This commitment prepares us to handle the claims of errors and contradictions that come. We know that our Bible will not have errors and contradictions. This is not to say that our Bible is free of difficulties (see 2 Peter 3:16). It is to say that no difficulty that we encounter within the Scripture requires us to modify our doctrine of Scripture. It is important to remember that we do not form our doctrine of Scripture from the difficulties we encounter. We form our doctrine of Scripture from the statements of the Scripture itself, and then we proceed to explore the difficulties.

A second basic consideration concerns what is required for some statement or statements of Scripture to rise to the level of an error or contradiction. According to A. A. Hodge and B. B. Warfield, not fewer than three criteria must be met before we admit the presence of an error in the Scripture.

Let it (1) be proved that each alleged discrepant statement certainly occurred in the original autograph
of the sacred book in which it is said to be found.
(2) Let it be proved that the interpretation which
occasions the apparent discrepancy is the one which
the passage was evidently intended to bear. It is not
sufficient to show a difficulty, which may spring out
of our defective knowledge of the circumstances.
The true meaning must be definitely and certainly
ascertained, and then shown to be irreconcilable
with other known truth. (3) Let it be proved that the
true sense of some part of the original autograph
is directly and necessarily inconsistent with some
certainly-known fact of history or truth of science,
or some other statement of Scripture certainly ascertained and interpreted.[38]

In other words, any statement in which an error is
alleged to occur must be in the original text of Scripture,
must be correctly interpreted, and must be proven to contradict a known fact from the world or another correctly
interpreted text of Scripture. This is the burden that those
who allege errors and contradictions in the Scripture must
shoulder. What Hodge and Warfield said in the nineteenth
century applies equally in the twenty-first century: "We
believe that it can be shown that this has never yet been
successfully done in the case of one single alleged instance
of error in the Word of God."[39]

Many fine evangelical books and commentaries give
concerted attention to addressing alleged errors and contradictions in the Bible. We will by no means try to replicate
their efforts. Here we may briefly note three things to keep
in mind as we encounter specific allegations of error in the

Bible.⁴⁰ First, a *difference* is not necessarily a *contradiction*.
Often, for instance, parallel accounts in the Gospels are not
identical. One gospel account records details or words that
are not present in another gospel account. This fact should
not disturb us. We expect independent accounts to differ in
their retelling of events and discussions. These differences
are part of the richness of the Gospels. Each gospel often
gives us a slightly different perspective from the others, and
one gospel may tell us more than another gospel's parallel
account. In fact, if parallel accounts in the Scripture were
uniform in detail, our suspicions might be raised. Such
uniformity might suggest to us collusion, which, in turn,
would cast doubt upon the historical worth of the accounts
in question. Our gospels therefore evidence not only their
richness as distinct accounts of our Lord, but in so doing
demonstrate their credibility as historical witnesses.

Second, the Bible may describe something without approv-
ing it. Both Testaments contain examples of the sinful words
and actions of individual persons. Sometimes these words and
actions go without much comment. This relative silence does not
constitute the Scripture's tacit or muted approval. For example,
Jacob marries two women and takes two more as concubines.
Readers of Genesis are sometimes dismayed that there is not
an explicit and immediate condemnation of the patriarch's
polygamy in that book. Yet the teaching of the Scripture is
clear in setting forth monogamy as the universal and abiding
standard for human beings (see Gen. 2:24 and Matt. 19:4–6).
Furthermore, it is clear from Genesis that Jacob's polygamy
results in a disordered and unhappy home. In this way Moses
implicitly disapproves of Jacob's departures from the law of
marriage instituted by God at the creation.

Third, and most important, it is the objector to inerrancy
and not the defender of inerrancy who shoulders the burden

of proof. Why is this so? It is because there is a cogent, rational case for inerrancy. Its premises are true, its reasoning
is valid, and therefore its conclusion commands assent. The
objector must demonstrate that a contradiction necessarily
and unavoidably exists either between two passages of Scripture properly interpreted or between a passage of Scripture
properly interpreted and a properly interpreted fact external
to the Scripture. By this standard, what appear to be contradictions turn out not to be contradictions at all. It may be that the
objector has misread or misinterpreted a certain passage of
Scripture, a fact of history, or a fact of science. It may be that
the objector has demonstrated a possible but not a necessary
contradiction. There may be, in fact, several possible ways to
resolve the difficulty that the objector brings forward. The
defender of inerrancy does not even have to commit to one
possible resolution or another. All that he is obligated to do
is to show that no contradiction is required.

Perhaps we may understand why two passages of Scripture will never contradict one another. An inerrant book
cannot contain statements that necessarily contradict
one another. But why may we be confident that a properly
interpreted statement of Scripture will never contradict a
properly interpreted fact of, say, science? The answer, as
J. I. Packer notes, is that "since the same God is the Author
both of nature and of Scripture, true science and a right
interpretation of Scripture cannot conflict."[41] We need to
explore, Packer continues, whether "appearance of contradiction is not due to mistakes and arbitrary assumptions,
both scientific and theological, which a closer scrutiny of
the evidence will enable us to correct," and to take heed of
"discounting one or other set of facts or . . . locking them
into two separate compartments in our minds and refusing
to bring them together."[42] This process is not an easy one

and will not yield immediate results. Whether or not we are able to reconcile these difficulties to the satisfaction of all parties concerned, we may be confident that God's "two books"—nature and Scripture—will never contradict one another.

A FINAL WORD

We have devoted time and effort to exploring what the Bible has to say about itself. We have been particularly concerned to come to terms with what the Bible means when it claims that it is inspired and inerrant. It is worth reminding ourselves why such an exercise is important. To put it simply, our view of the Bible makes a world of difference for the way we live in the here and now. Is the Bible simply a collection of the fallible responses of men of old to the revelation of God? Then the Bible does not give me God's Word. I am left to my own devices to search out whether God has revealed himself or not, and whether a sinner like me can be saved. Is the Bible a mixture of God's infallible words and men's fallible words? Then, absent an infallible measure of God's infallible words in the Bible, I can never be certain what it is that God has spoken in the Scripture. Agonizing uncertainty about the state of my soul before God is the best I can hope for in this life.

Or is the Bible the holy, inspired, infallible, and inerrant Word of God? Then I can be sure that every word of the Bible has proceeded from God's mouth. I can be sure it is a thoroughly reliable and authoritative guide for what I must believe and what I must do in order to be saved. With unqualified confidence in the Bible's author, I can be sure that I am no fool for committing the welfare of my eternal soul to its teaching. Whatever error or deception I encounter from the world, from Satan, or from my own heart, I have an infallible Bible to expose that lie and to guide me in all truth. When the Bible condemns a sin that presses hard upon me and entices me, I may be sure that it is worth it to battle mightily against that sin. When betrayal, rejection, deep disappointment, illness, grief, and death itself invade my life, I can be absolutely sure that the solace, blessedness, and hope that this book offers to me through Jesus Christ is true and real.

What you and I believe about the Bible matters. We should thank God that he has given us the Bible that he has given us, and has given us firm assurance of its utter truthfulness. When you and I understand what the Bible really is, then we will say with the psalmist, "The law of your mouth is better to me than thousands of gold and silver pieces" (Ps. 119:72).

FOR FURTHER READING

Hodge, A. A., and B. B. Warfield. *Inspiration*. 1881; repr., Grand Rapids: Baker, 1979.

Nichols, Stephen J., and Eric T. Brandt. *Ancient Word, Changing Worlds: The Doctrine of Scripture in a Modern Age*. Wheaton, IL: Crossway, 2009.

Packer, J. I. *"Fundamentalism" and the Word of God*. Grand Rapids: Eerdmans, 1958.

———. *God Has Spoken*. Downers Grove, IL: InterVarsity Press, 1979.

Sproul, R.C. *Scripture Alone: The Evangelical Doctrine*. Phillipsburg, NJ: P&R, 2005.

Warfield, B. B. *Revelation and Inspiration*. 1932; repr., Grand Rapids: Baker, 2000.

NOTES

1 J. I. Packer, *God Has Spoken* (Downers Grove, IL: InterVarsity Press, 1979), 28–30.

2   Louis Berkhof, *Introductory Volume to Systematic Theology* (Grand Rapids: Eerdmans, 1932), 117.

3   B. B. Warfield, "The Idea of Revelation and Theories of Revelation," in *The Works of Benjamin B. Warfield*, 10 vols. (New York: Oxford University Press, 1932), 1:37.

4   See the Westminster Confession of Faith, 1.1.

5   "Christianity and Revelation," in *B. B. Warfield: Selected Shorter Writings*, ed. John E. Meeter, 2 vols. (Phillipsburg, NJ: P&R, 1970, 1973), 1:27.

6   In saying "ordinarily," we mean that God is quite capable of saving people whose minds are either too immature (infants) or too damaged (the mentally handicapped) to understand the contents of special revelation. See here Westminster Confession of Faith, 10.3.

7   The theologian B. B. Warfield has a helpful taxonomy of biblical revelation. There is "external manifestation"—the "mighty works by which God makes Himself known," and there is "internal suggestion"—prophecy, visions, and dreams. There is, lastly, "concursive operation"—what we see in "an inspired psalm or epistle or history" in which the Holy Spirit "works in, with, and through" the human writers "to communicate to the product qualities distinctly superhuman." "The Biblical Idea of Revelation," in *Works*, 1:15.

8   Strictly speaking, we should think even of this interpretative redemptive word as a redemptive act!

9   Westminster Confession of Faith, 1.2.

10 See Packer, *God Has Spoken*, 32–35.

11 See the technical discussion of Warfield, "Inspiration," *Works*, 1:77–81.

12 Packer, *God Has Spoken*, 98.

13 Warfield, "Inspiration," *Selected Shorter Writings*, 2:615. Elsewhere, Warfield insists that inspiration is a "mode" of revelation; *Works*, 1:106–7.

14 Some understand "prophecy" here in an even broader sense—the whole of the Old Testament Scripture.

15 Warfield, "Inspiration," *Works*, 1:82.

16 To learn more about the reasons why Christians have acknowledged the twenty-seven books of the New Testament to be canonical, see

Warfield, "The Formation of the Canon of the New Testament," *Works*, 1:451–56.

17 These two examples come from Warfield, "The Authority and Inspiration of the Scriptures," *Selected Shorter Writings*, 2:539.

18 See, for instance, the passages cited at Warfield, "Inspiration," *Selected Shorter Writings*, 1:32–33; "Authority and Inspiration," *Selected Shorter Writings*, 2:634–35; and Berkhof, *Systematic Theology*, 146–50.

19 R. C. Sproul, *Scripture Alone: The Evangelical Doctrine* (Phillipsburg, NJ: P&R, 2005), 136.

20 See Article VI of the Chicago Statement on Biblical Inerrancy (1978), quoted in ibid.

21 J. I. Packer, *"Fundamentalism" and the Word of God* (Grand Rapids: Eerdmans, 1958), 77.

22 Ibid., 82.

23 Packer, *God Has Spoken*, 100.

24 A. A. Hodge, *Outlines of Theology*, (1879; repr. Edinburgh: Banner of Truth, 1972), 68.

25 Packer, *God Has Spoken*, 100–101.

26 Warfield, "The Divine and the Human in the Bible," *Selected Shorter Writings*, 2:546.

27 Warfield, "Inspiration," *Works*, 1:96.

28 See the discussion at Stephen J. Nichols and Eric T. Brandt, *Ancient Word, Changing Worlds: The Doctrine of Scripture in a Modern Age* (Wheaton, IL: Crossway, 2009), 91–92.

29 Packer, *God Has Spoken*, 111.

30 John Frame, *The Doctrine of the Word of God* (Phillipsburg, NJ: P&R, 2010), 533.

31 The phrase is that of Robert D. Preus, "Notes on the Inerrancy of Scripture," quoted in Nichols and Brandt, *Ancient Word*, 89.

32 John H. Gerstner, *Primitive Theology: The Collected Primers of John H. Gerstner* (Morgan, PA: Soli Deo Gloria, 1996), 87, 89.

33 E. J. Young, *Thy Word Is Truth*, 123, quoted in Nichols and Brandt, *Ancient Word*, 94.

34 A. T. B. McGowan, *The Divine Spiration of Scripture: Challenging Evangelical Perspectives* (Nottingham, UK: Apollos, 2007), 114.

35 McGowan appears to adopt the former alternative when he claims that inerrancy is not a "legitimate implication" of the doctrine of inspiration, 115.

24

36 Quoted in Berkhof, *Systematic Theology*, 161.

37 We have presented in this booklet only a portion of the full case for the Bible as the Word of God, limiting ourselves to demonstrating the Scripture's teaching about itself as divine revelation, the inspired and inerrant Word of God. The classic Reformed expression of this full case may be found in the articles in Volume 1 (*Revelation and Inspiration*) of *The Works of Benjamin B. Warfield*.

38 A. A. Hodge and B. B. Warfield, *Inspiration* (1881; repr., Grand Rapids: Baker, 1979), 36.

39 Ibid.

40 The first two are mentioned in Berkhof, *Systematic Theology*, 161–62.

41 Packer, *Fundamentalism*, 135.

42 Ibid.

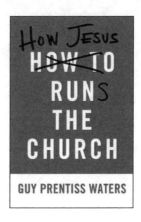

Few books on church leadership explore the biblical foundations of church government. This one does—providing pastors, elders, students, and laypeople with a greater understanding of what the church is and how it should be governed.

Waters also examines the offices that Jesus has appointed in the church and investigates how elders in particular are to serve her.

"It is a pleasure to commend Guy Waters's book as a sound, biblical, accessible guide to the nature of the church. Written by a churchman for the church, it can be read with profit by office-bearers, Sunday school teachers, and any believer who wants a deeper grasp of what it means to be a member of Christ's church on earth."
  —**Carl R. Trueman**, Professor of Historical Theology and
    Church History, Westminster Theological Seminary

ALSO IN THE
BASICS OF THE FAITH SERIES

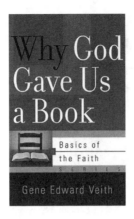

This booklet by Gene Edward Veith is a clear, concise examination of biblical authority and inerrancy and a scholarly but readable defense of the sufficiency of Scripture. Learn why and how the church should continue to defend the truths of the Bible.

Basics of the Faith booklets introduce readers to basic Reformed doctrine and practice. On issues of church government and practice they reflect that framework—otherwise they are suitable for all church situations.

OTHER TITLES IN THE SERIES INCLUDE:
What is a True Calvinist? Philip Graham Ryken
What is a Reformed Church? Stephen Smallman
What is True Conversion? Stephen Smallman
What is the Lord's Supper? Richard D. Philips
What is the Christian Worldview? Philip Graham Ryken
What Are Election and Predestination? Richard D. Philips
How Our Children Come to Faith, Stephen Smallman
Why Do We Baptize Infants? Bryan Chapell
What Is Justification by Faith Alone? J. V. Fesko
How Do We Glorify God? John D. Hannah

MORE ON THE BIBLE
FROM P&R PUBLISHING

JAMES M. BOICE

EDMUND P. CLOWNEY

MARK DEVER

J. LIGON DUNCAN III

J. I. PACKER

RICHARD D. PHILLIPS

PHILIP GRAHAM RYKEN

R.C. SPROUL

Here the Philadelphia Conference on Reformed Theology explores the Author's glory by unfolding the richness and perfection of the Bible. In essays collected from the best addresses on the subject, eight of the top pastor-scholars of the past thirty years share their insight and answers.